Designing with light on paper and film

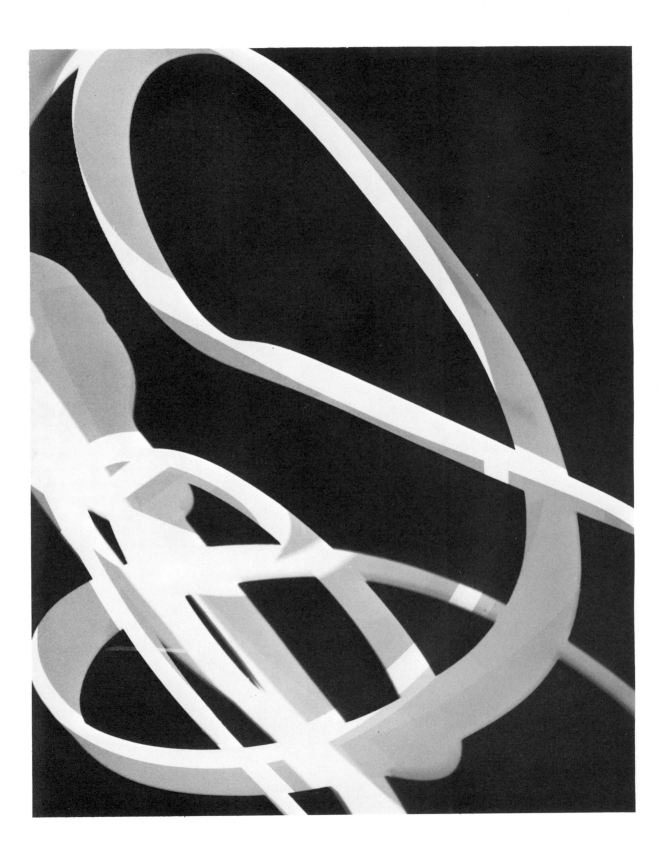

Designing with light
on paper and film

Robert W. Cooke
Professor of Art
Paterson State College
Wayne, *New Jersey*

Davis Publications, Inc., Worcester, Massachusetts

Dedication   This book is dedicated to the memory of one whose remarkable intellect as a teacher and compassion as a person combined to form a lasting influence upon countless scores of her students: Miss Rosemary Ketcham, pioneer in the teaching of design.   With keen aesthetic perception Miss Ketcham formulated foundational and advanced studies of design and color which she taught with expectations that demanded the best efforts of her students.   For many years after founding the Department of Design at the University of Kansas, Miss Ketcham inspired her students to develop their sensitivities; many of these students, in turn, have sought to inspire others.

Consulting editors: Sarita R. Rainey and George F. Horn

Copyright 1969   Davis Publications, Inc., Worcester, Massachusetts
Library of Congress catalog card number: 75–75730
SBN: 87192-030-1   Second Printing 1972
Printing: Davis Press, Inc.   *Type:* Univers   *Design:* Panagiota Darras
Front cover and title page photos: Judy Stolk Malinchak
Back cover photo: Pauline Albenda

Preface

Designs with light may be made without a camera from objects placed directly on photo-sensitive surfaces of paper, film or glass. The term "photogram" (light drawing) has been long employed to refer to direct methods as well as to the occasional use of a contact printer or enlarger in a darkroom. Whichever method is used, objects are selected for the design with consideration for their characteristics under light and arranged or projected on the photosensitive surface. Development of the print follows.

In this book the subject of light designs is treated in a comprehensive manner which includes techniques and processes both traditional and contemporary; the latter include making designs in roomlight and with some non-photographic techniques.

Adventure and intrigue await the experimenter in design as he improvises with line, form, texture and sometimes with color, for the aesthetic delights he can create. The inherent feature of designing with light is the freedom to improvise, to invent subject matter and to produce an art form in the contemporary idiom.

Designing with Light will be of special significance to persons who are interested in design experiences as doer-experimenter, teacher-innovator or viewer-appreciator. Teachers of children and youth will find ideas and suggestions here for creative activities in making light designs as will instructors of college students and the advanced amateur, all of whom are interested in developing natural aesthetic abilities. Methods and techniques for making light designs range from simple to relatively complicated; all of them may be challenging. The selection of activities by teachers of children for use in the classroom should be made with regard not only to age levels, but with consideration for the interests and abilities of children and youth. The capabilities of young children should not be underestimated, for fertile imaginations can invent techniques to create endless designs with roomlight handling materials. Older children and youth, who are capable of more advanced techniques, will find working with basic photographic equipment in the darkroom to be of particular interest. In all activities for creating light designs, in and out of the classroom, it is to be urged that the fascination for aesthetically pleasing results be the prime motivation.

The author had no intention of writing a "how to do it" book. Rather, it may be said in another cliche that he has attempted to write a "do-it-yourself" book. Techniques are briefly described for their informational value in the hope that the reader may feel creative intrigue to conduct his own adventures in making prints and transparencies. Important as techniques are, they should not be the end in creative activities, only the means; the end is the expression of one's own ideas, one's self.

I wish to express my gratitude to Mr. Christian Schad for reading Section I and to Mr. Peter Bunnell, Associate Curator, Department of Photography, The Museum of Modern

Art, New York, for his assistance in locating information and for making available a print from his personal collection.

Two former students in my class Design With Photography have contributed significantly to this book. Judy Stolk Malinchak executed many printings in and out of the photo lab. Both she and Francine Raia Buss worked with their students to discover additional techniques for roomlight printing. I am indebted to many of my students and to other persons, noted elsewhere, who generously gave their permission to use prints and transparencies.

Sincere appreciation is extended to Miss Sarita Rainey who was receptive to the idea which resulted in this book. Unfailing companion on research trips and typist was my wife, Lucile, to whom I say, "Merci beaucoup!"

R. W. C.

Foreword

Sensitivity to design has long been a concern of the art teacher. "Designing With Light" offers an extra dimension to any well-rounded art program by encouraging exploration and lively student participation. This is especially noticeable in the primary and middle schools where inventive and curious young minds can use shadow, reflection, and translucent effects in a wide range of creative ways. And the surprises inherent in this activity will trigger the interest of students in special education. High school and college students, too, will discover unlimited possibilities to improvise in this visual medium.

Making designs with light dates from the early 1800's when experimental prints were made during the development of the photographic process; today the technique is being revived and expanded as an art form. Designing with light can stimulate innovative thinking as combinations of light sources, and materials and techniques to create designs are considered for experimentation. However, a potential is not enough; the designer-student must experiment with different materials, various arrangements and degrees of light, and use them all in sensitive and disciplined ways as he composes.

Robert W. Cooke, a design specialist who has broad experience as a teacher at all levels of education, is professor of art at Paterson State College, Wayne, New Jersey. He is well aware of the central role of designing experiences in the aesthetic growth and development of students. In this book he presents an imaginative and stimulating array of materials which provide the reader with refreshing insights into this always interesting—often dramatic art medium. Through discussions of design, materials, processes and suggested experiments, Dr. Cooke encourages the reader with exciting sources of inspiration, plus helpful techniques for the beginner and the advanced amateur.

Sarita R. Rainey
Supervisor of Art, Montclair Public Schools, New Jersey

Contents

8

1 William Henry Fox Talbot: Photogenic Drawing (Flowers), 1839. The Metropolitan Museum of Art, New York City, Harris Brisbane Dick Fund, 1936

2 (right) William Henry Fox Talbot: A Photographic Engraving Made Without a Camera, c. 1852. Collection The Museum of Modern Art, New York City

A history of light designs (photograms)

Of the many developments in the history of photography there are two which are of particular significance to light designs. First, in 1802, Thomas Wedgwood, son of the English potter, in collaboration with Humphry Davy, made *direct* prints of botanical specimens, lace and paintings on glass which had been positioned on white paper or leather that had been charged with silver nitrate, then exposed to sunlight. These prints could not be viewed in ordinary light because no means to neutralize the development had been devised. Second, in 1839, also in England, William Henry Fox Talbot[1] made "photogenic drawings" of plants (Print 1) in which he used the camera obscura, a device using a mirror to reflect the subject in a ground glass, an indirect method. Later he invented a direct method of printmaking in engraving (Print 2) which he patented c. 1852.[2] These developments in photography are of importance to light designs, Wedgwood's for the process of printing with light on a sensitized surface and Talbot's for the utilization of a light-produced image; the direct process which both men used to project objects in silhouette with light is in the manner of making today's photographic light designs.

For almost all of i s early history photography was marked with steady technical progress rather than with expanding the interpretation of subject matter. The latter included the recording of portraits, scenes, architecture and events. The purpose of photography and the concern of photographers was to record a subject as the camera saw it: to report with objective realism, which may be termed "documentary." This is not to say that photographs made during this period were without aesthetic or artistic merit; rather, the reference is to the primary intent of photographers.

The first works in making abstract and non-objective photographic prints were done by photographer-artists of great imagination who were influenced by new directions in painting, for example: cubism, vorticism, dadaism and futurism. Alvin Langdon Coburn

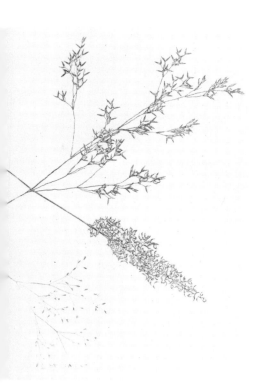

[1] Talbot also is recognized for the process he later discovered to neutralize the developer, the printing of photographs on paper (Daguerre and some other inventors printed on metal while still others printed on glass), the use of a negative which permitted for the first time the making of positive prints, and spark photography (stop-action).

[2] "Talbot coated a metal plate with a bichromated gelatin emulsion. The sprigs (see Print 2) were flattened against the emulsion with glass and exposed to sunlight. After removing the sprigs the plate was washed in cold water to remove the unexposed, unhardened emulsion. The plate was then etched in a platinum dichloride solution, after which the remaining gelatin was sponged off. It was then inked, wiped and printed."—Eugene Ostroff, Curator of Photography, Smithsonian Institution, Washington, D.C. (Letter, July 10, 1968).

10

3 *Alvin Langdon Coburn: Vortograph, 1917. Collection of Peter C. Bunnell, New York City*

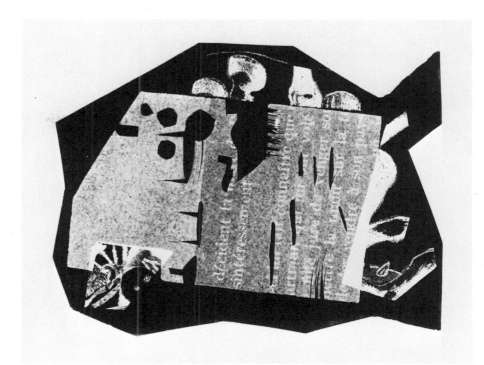

4 Christian Schad: Schadograph, 1918; Permission the Artist.   Collection The Museum of Modern Art, New York City.   Anonymous Gift

was the first photographer (with the possible exception of Eugene Atget) whose work emphasized aesthetic content of the subject, including expressive elements, rather than singularly recording descriptive content.   Examples of his approach to photography are included in his well known series of photographs made from buildings and towers high above the streets, sidewalks and parks of New York City.   Many of these photographs were flat patterns in values and textures which abstracted the subject matter; this series titled ''New York from Its Pinnacles'' was shown in London in the Goupil Gallery in 1913. In 1917 Coburn exhibited the first purely non-objective photographs, also in London, in the Camera Club.   In this exhibition Coburn showed thirteen paintings and eighteen ''Vortographs,'' the term adapted from vorticism by Ezra Pound for these prints made by arranging selected objects which were reflected in three mirrors and photographed (Print 3.)   Coburn had found a new and personal subject matter for the camera.

Using methods which were basically the same as Talbot's, the Dadists Christian Schad (Print 4) in Geneva in 1918, and Man Ray (Print 5) in Paris in 1921, as well as Laszlo Maholy-Nagy (Print 6) in Berlin, also in 1921, made photographic prints by working *directly* on light sensitive papers and films.   No cameras were used!   Schad called his prints, made with two-dimensional objects, ''schadographs,'' the term derived from his name by Tristan Tzara; while Maholy-Nagy and Ray called their prints, which included three-dimensional objects, ''photograms'' and ''rayograms,'' respectively; all three men were painters.   The techniques used by these early innovators were similar in that they composed their designs with objects which were carefully selected for their properties under light.   Some of these objects were opaque, some translucent while others fractured the light and projected their own patterns.   The light source which exposed the paper, film or glass slide was often moved during exposure to produce repetition in the design. The resulting prints were personal aesthetic statements, essentially non-objective; many of them were untitled.

5 (opposite) Man Ray: Rayograph (Print from portfolio: Man Ray 12 Rayograms, 1921–1923, Stuttgart, Paris, 1963); Permission the Artist. George Eastman House Collection, Rochester, New York

6 Laszlo Maholy-Nagy. Photogram, 1926; Permission Sibyl Maholy-Nagy. George Eastman House Collection, Rochester, New York

13

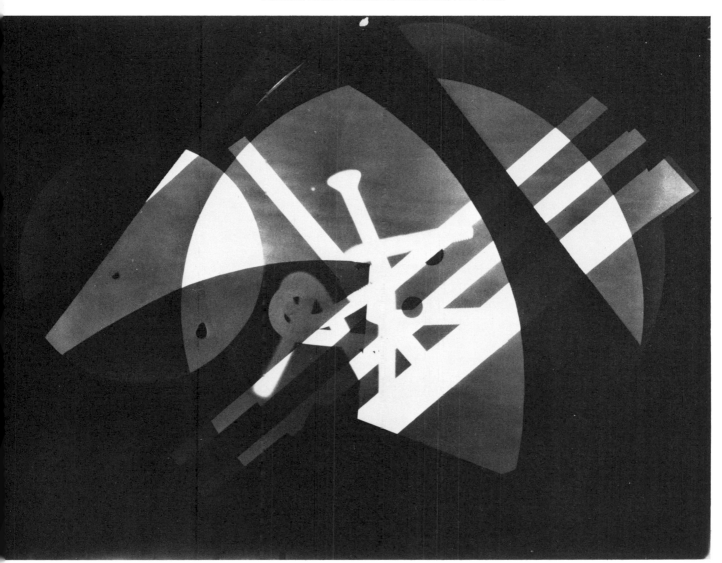

14

7 *Francis Bruguiere: Untitled, 1932; Permission Rosalinde Fuller, M.B.E. George Eastman House Collection, Rochester, New York*

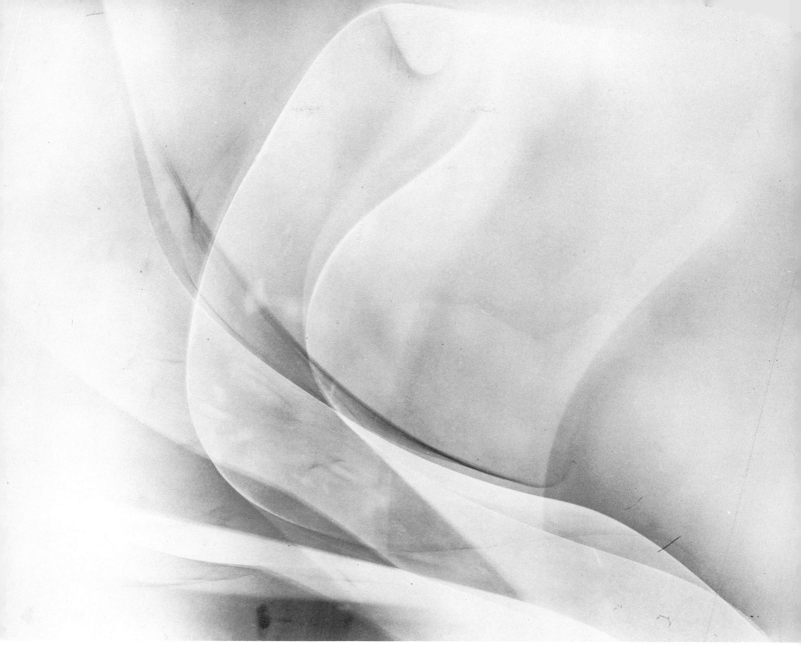

8 Lotte Jacobi: One of a series of photogenics, 1948–1959; Permission the Artist; Collection The Museum of Modern Art, New York City

On the subject of "Creative Photography" the photographer Francis Bruguiere (Print 7)[3] wrote: "It is possible for photographers to make or design objects that can be treated with light, thereby creating a world of their own . . ."[4] In creating this "world of their own" artist-photographers had also created a new art form: light designs.

Continuing in the best tradition of creative photographer-artist we note the imaginative works of Lotte Jacobi (Print 8), Gyorgy Kepes (Print 9) and Henry W. Ray (Print 10.)

[3]Light designs may also be made with overlaid and multi-exposed negatives.
[4]Nathan Lyons, Ed., *Photographers on Photography.* Englewood Cliffs, New Jersey, Prentice-Hall, Inc., 1966, p. 35.

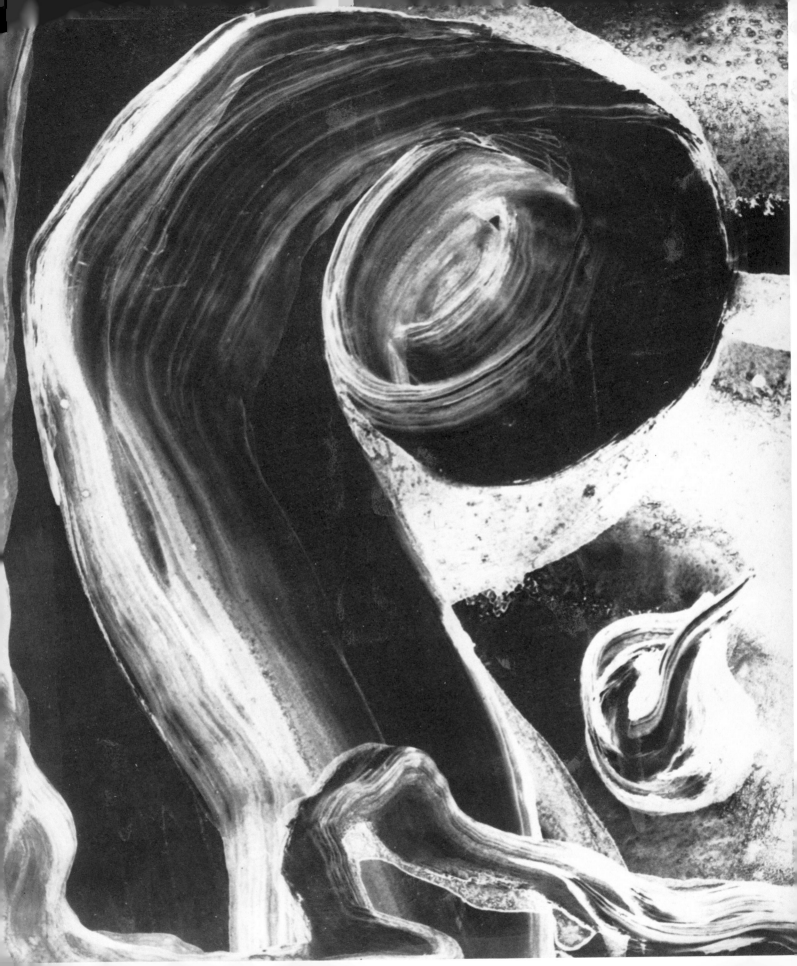

9 (opposite) Gyorgy Kepes: Abstraction ⚹ 3, 1939; Permission the Artist.   Collection The Museum of Modern Art, New York City

10 Henry W. Ray: Soot Patterned ⚹ 2, 1968; Permission the Artist.   Collection of the Author

Some guidelines for composing light designs

Whatever one may be attempting to say or to express in light designs, his efforts may prove to be more satisfying if they are guided by a working knowledge of underlying visual design elements. The study of the work of photographer-artists will prove to be enlightening by observing the many ways they employ design elements. As one makes prints and transparencies he should study his own efforts for successes and failures in design. Perhaps it is best to work (compose) intuitively with the resolution of design questions coming more from *feeling* one's way (study may condition feeling.) When reviewing one's work for its strengths and weaknesses, *thinking* and evaluation become necessary for improvement and growth.

What is design? Basically design is the arrangement of objects in space. One of the first considerations in design is *visual balance* of which there are two kinds: one kind is called formal or symmetrical and refers to those designs which have the same forms on either side of an imaginary center line passing through the design area from top to bottom. Informal or asymmetrical balance has different forms on either side of the imaginary center line; however, visual balance is still achieved. Of the two kinds of balance the latter is usually considered to be more subtle and sophisticated.

To produce a feeling of order in design it is desirable to have a *center of interest* or point of visual emphasis. The center of interest may be the largest form in the design with the greatest amount of black or white (or the brightest color.) A center of interest is most often placed well within the design area and away from edges and corners of the print or transparency. A design may have secondary points of emphasis which complement the center of interest by reinforcing and repeating it while not competing with it. Around the center of interest are placed other lines, forms and textures (and colors) in different values (lights and darks) to complete the arrangement of objects in the design area.

Variety and contrast are the "seasoning" of design and may be compared to the use of salt and pepper in the preparation of food. A selected variety of lines, forms and textures with values (and colors) provide the contrasts which enliven and make more dynamic the print or transparency.

Repetition of some of the parts of the design tends to hold a design together. Repetition is necessary in creating good design but too much of it can result in redundancy. For example, with the repetition of a dominant shape or color in other areas and on a smaller scale, the design may assume internal relatedness or integrity. Repetitions must always be planned in subtle ways to create a harmonious design.

Overlapping parts of a print or transparency tends to build stability in a design. Only some of the parts need to overlap to avoid a monotonous condition. Parts should not come too close to each other or overlap at points which make for distractions and possibly create conflicting centers of interest.

Important design considerations discussed here are: balance, a center of interest, variety and contrast, repetition and overlapping. When all of these visual elements are successfully put together in a design, the result will have the quality of *unity*. All parts of the design work together when unity has been achieved. A good test is to ask yourself the following questions: "What should be taken out of this design?" and "What should be added to this design?" When the answer to both questions can be "Nothing" you may have achieved unity in the design.

When the visual elements of a design work together, the result should be an intangible 'rightness" which reflects the taste of its originator.

In making light designs the mastery of basic technical skills is necessary to provide a vehicle for the better expression of one's creative ideas. Marjorie Elliott Bevlin[1] stated it this way: "The fine line between good technical photography and outstanding achievement is crossed only by the photographer with creative ability, with the eye and soul of an artist, and understanding that light, that essential of any photograph, can be his most valuable ally in design."

No other two-dimensional art form so readily lends itself to working directly with the visual design elements as does the medium of light designs.

[1] Bevlin, Marjorie Elliott, *Design Through Discovery*, New York, New York, Holt, Rinehart and Winston, 1963, p. 360.

11 (below-left) Students planning light designs with various materials for roomlight printing; note trays for chemicals.

12 Students making light designs with selected objects for roomlight printing; note photoflood lamp, at top of picture, for exposing paper.

Light designs with paper

Light designs may be made with only a few materials and the simplest of equipment. Guided by a sense of adventure one can produce prints expressing design-ideas in a medium which invites innovation. Particularly uncomplicated is the making of light designs in ordinary *roomlight* for which the following materials and equipment are needed:

Materials

selected items with which to compose designs
papers: A1, R1, AT1 (Kodagraph)[1]
solutions: Kodak Dektol or Kodagraph developer
        stop bath
        fixer

Equipment

one reflector photoflood lamp (375 watts)
an extension cord with a lamp socket and a clamp
a timer, watch or clock
three plastic or enameled trays, 8" x 10" or larger, for solutions
three plastic or bamboo tongs (one of each solution)
a large tray or sink in which to rinse prints
glass bottles, ½ gallon or larger, in which to store solutions

Light designs may be composed with two- or three-dimensional objects which may be transparent, opaque or translucent and of unlimited variety in shape, size and texture. Practically any materials may be used; however, two-dimensional objects as paper, gauze, thin wood pieces and sheet metal scraps are some of the best for first attempts. These items may be placed directly upon light sensitive papers, in a contact printer or in an enlarger. Three-dimensional objects such as shaped paper, a glass ash tray, hands and plastic or metal objects may also be placed directly upon the paper with the light source penetrating the form or casting shadows which change from sharp to soft outlines. Combining two- and three-dimensional objects adds interest to the design. For suggestions in arranging the design see "Some Guidelines for Composing Light Designs."

A light source with which to project the design and expose the photosensitive surface of paper (or film) is needed. This light source may be any one of a variety of white light

[1]These papers are available from Business Systems Markets Division, Eastman Kodak Company, Rochester, N.Y. 14650.

21

13 *(left) Student light designs, some on glass sheets, ready to be exposed.*

14 *(right) Objects arranged on R1 paper for roomlight printing of light design. A glass sheet (edges taped), holds objects in place for contact print; objects may also be placed on the glass.*

types ranging from a photoflood lamp to a single match or the conventional contact printer and enlarger. The intensity of the light source is relative to the density of the objects selected for making the design, distance to the paper, sensitivity of the paper, length of time for the exposure and other variables as may be present. Experimentation and experience will provide calculations for exposures with increasing accuracy. The captions which accompany prints have information for making light designs including the type of paper, distance to light source and length of time for exposure. For example: R1 paper, photoflood lamp at 37 ½'' for one minute.

Roomlight printing

When working with photographic materials it may be expected that a darkroom is necessary. It is possible, however, to work in roomlight when using papers and films of low sensitivity to normal indoor lighting conditions, for a short period of time. Some of these materials are the papers A1, R1 and AT1 which were used to produce the light designs illustrated in this section.

In Prints 11 and 12, students are selecting materials for their designs which are placed on individual sheets of glass (edges taped), then moved to a position on the paper. These materials include wire, coins, balsa wood strips, roll of tape, yarn, plastic strip, cardboard, reed and a square brass piece as illustrated in Prints 13 and 14. Exposure of the R1 paper by one photoflood lamp at thirty inches for sixty seconds (Print 15) is followed by students' placing the exposed paper in the developing solution (Print 16). Three solutions and three trays are used, as shown in Print 17. The arrangement of trays and solutions is as follows:

Tray No. 1	Tray No. 2	Tray No. 3
Developer	Stop Bath	Fixer

The developer may be Kodak Dektol or Kodagraph, the stop bath is 28% acetic acid (1 ½ ounces to 32 ounces of water) and Kodak fixer. Directions for mixing the developers and the fixer are on their respective containers. All solutions are used at the temperature of about 68°F. Now to develop the print: Slip the exposed paper face up into the developer, keeping it under the surface and gently agitating it with tongs. Traces of the design should emerge in a few seconds and in about ten to fifteen seconds it should be ready to remove. Using tongs hold the print by one corner over the developer and allow it to drip, then quickly slip it into the stop bath solution for five seconds. Use different tongs in each tray so as not to mix solutions. Place the print in the fixer solution for ten minutes with frequent

agitation. Finally, wash the print by placing it in a large tray of cool running water for thirty minutes; move prints around to insure thorough washing. Tray siphons may be purchased for washing prints or water from the faucet may run into a glass tumbler and overflow into the tray not contacting the prints directly. Dry the print by laying it on paper towels or blotters or use an electric dryer. When dry, the print may be mounted on cardboard with rubber cement or by using dry mount tissue and an electric iron.

The light designs illustrated in Prints 18 through 34 were made in roomlight conditions with four different white light sources: photoflood lamp, slide projector, fluorescent lamp and contact printer. Descriptive information for each illustration is included in the captions.

23

15 (above-left) Students exposing their light designs with photoflood lamp in roomlight, while the author offers suggestions.

16 (left) Students developing light designs in roomlight.

17 (below-right) Student with prints in stop bath (center tray) and fixer solutions (right tray) following exposure by photoflood lamp and development (left tray).

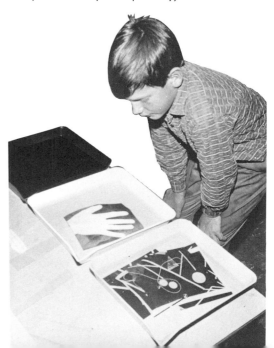

18/19 Light designs exposed with a photoflood lamp at 30'' for 60 seconds on R1, and developed.

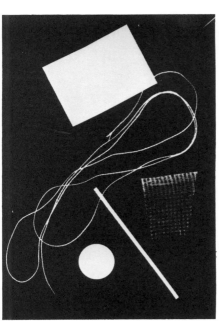

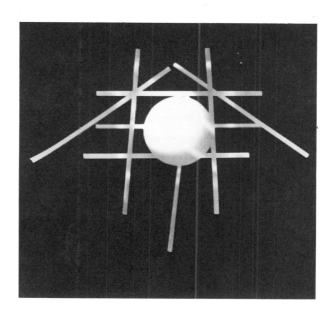

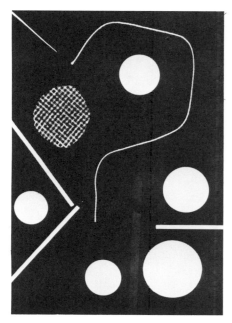

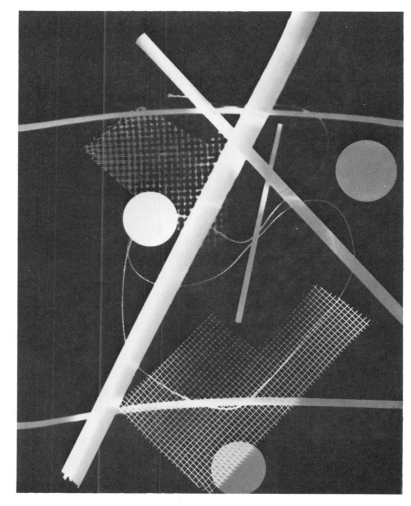

20/21/22/23 Light designs exposed with a photoflood lamp at 30'' for 60 seconds, on R1, and developed.

24 *(left) Light designs printed on AT1 paper with a slide projector as the source of white light, at 36'' for 1 ½ minutes and developed in Kodagraph.*

25/26/27/28 *Light designs printed on AT1 paper with ceiling fluorescent light as the source of white light, at 6 feet for 11 minutes and developed in Kodagraph.*

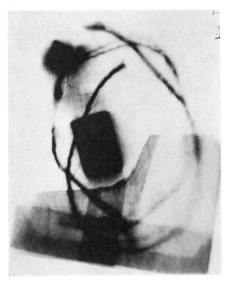

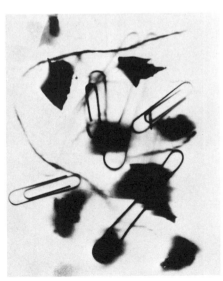

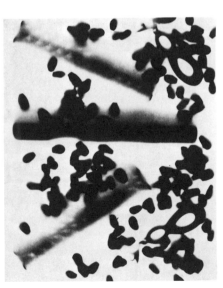

Light design printed on R1 paper with a photoflood lamp at 36" for 2 minutes and developed in Kodak Dektol.

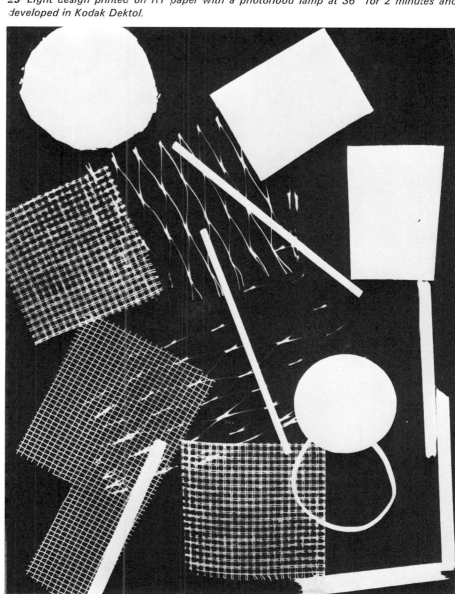

28

30/31/32 Three light designs printed on A1 paper with a photoflood lamp at 36'' for 3 minutes. Note the unusual effects created in the hand prints when fingers touched the paper or when they were moved during exposure.

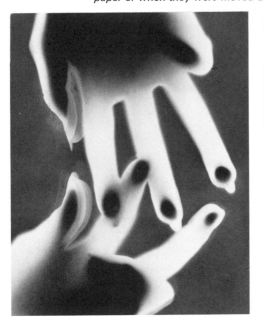

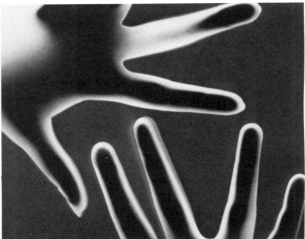

33 *(above) Light design printed on R1 with photoflood lamp at 37½'' for 1 minute and developed in Kodak Dektol.*

34 *(below) Torn paper design printed on R1 paper in a contact printer for 3 minutes and developed in Kodak Dektol.*

Darkroom printing The making of light design prints on paper in the darkroom can be done satisfactorily with minimal materials and equipment. However, it is possible to exercise more print control to produce a greater range in values, for example, by using an enlarger than by using a white 60 watt light bulb to expose the paper. The following materials and equipment are needed depending upon the selection of techniques:

Materials selected items with which to compose designs, two- and three-dimensional
papers: Velour VB-R2 (DuPont)
         Medalist F2 (Kodak)
solutions: Kodak Dektol or Kodagraph developer
         stop bath
         fixer

Equipment one 60 watt white light bulb, contact printing frame or a contact printer or an enlarger,
an extension cord with a lamp socket and a clamp
timer, watch or clock
three plastic or enameled trays, 8'' x 10'' or larger, for solutions
three plastic or bamboo tongs (one for each solution)
a large tray or sink in which to rinse prints
glass bottles, ½ gallon or larger, in which to store solutions

     When working with photographic papers in the darkroom, all white light must be excluded and a colored lamp, such as a 60 watt yellow (bug) light or a regular safelight, must be used; white light would expose or fog the papers when they are removed from their wrappers.

     Papers used for contact and enlarger prints are of two types. Contact papers (silver chloride) are used close to the light source; therefore, these papers are slower, or less sensitive, than projection papers (silver bromide) used in an enlarger farther from the light source. Papers of both types are available in several grades which refer to the matching contrast of negatives, which are not often used in making light designs. Number two (normal

contrast) grade will give good results in either contact or enlarging papers. Papers are also available with different surface characteristics, for example: glossy, matte and lustre. Single and double weights (thickness) are also available. While there may be practical considerations in selecting surfaces and weights of papers for light designs, more important are the choices which reflect the personal taste of the designer.

Darkroom printing of papers in making light designs may be done in several ways. Using either a contact printing frame or a contact printer, the method may be the same as is used for making ordinary photographic prints. The frame is a simple device with a glass front and a removable back which permits the placement of flat items on the emulsion (slick) side of the contact paper, toward the glass. Exposure of the paper is done by placing the loaded frame one to two feet from a 60-watt white electric bulb which is turned on for a few seconds. The contact printer is a box with a glass top which contains a white bulb that is turned on for a few seconds during exposure. See Print 35. This device simplifies printing, is compact and makes it unnecessary to put away photographic papers in the darkroom during exposure as the printer is light-tight.

Another way to make light design prints on paper is with an enlarger. See Print 36. Objects to form the design are placed in the enlarger, its bulb is turned on and the design is projected onto the paper. With the use of the enlarger, considerable flexibility is possible as in the selection of only a part of the projected design for the print and in moving objects about while viewing the projected design, before exposing the paper. Two-dimensional or essentially flat objects are most suitable for the enlarger method of making light designs.

Darkroom printing may also be done without the use of either a contact printer or an enlarger as was described in roomlight printing. Selected objects, which may be three-dimensional, can be placed directly upon the paper and exposed with a variety of white light sources, some of which may be moved. Movement of objects or of the light source

35 (above-left) A contact printer, designed for making prints from negatives of the same size in the darkroom, is also used for making light designs in roomlight and in darkroom situations depending upon the materials selected. Note Prints 34 and 91. See Glossary.

36 (left) An enlarger, designed for making prints from a negative of a size smaller than that of the print, is also used for making light designs in the darkroom with two-dimensional and three-dimensional materials. For examples of the latter see Prints 38 and 44. See Glossary.

32

37 *Flowers and weeds were put between two glass sheets, placed in an enlarger and printed as a negative on Velour VB 2 paper. Exposures of 3 and 5 seconds were made, moving the paper between exposures; developed in Kodagraph.*

during exposure produces subtle, transparent-like forms with a variety of values (grays.)
Experimentation will determine the length of exposures which will usually range between four and ten seconds.

The development of prints made in the darkroom is the same process and may use the same chemical solutions as described for roomlight printing; see page 22 for this information. Versatol developer also may be used.

Prints 37 through 47 are illustrations of light designs created in the darkroom with various materials. These designs are unique both aesthetically and technically and have been made by persons representing a wide range in age and experience. It is suggested that each design be viewed and the aesthetic response which it invokes be noted. Reference to "Some Guidelines For Composing Light Designs" may assist in analyzing these responses.

38 Vaseline was arranged with fingers on a glass sheet, placed in an enlarger and printed on Medalist F2 paper with a 20 second exposure; developed in Selectol.

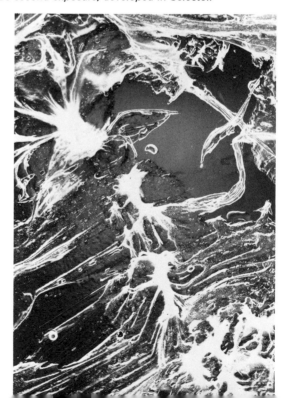

34

39 Four glass bottles, containing ink, were placed on Medalist F2 paper. With an enlarger (aperture f/8) lamp turned on, a magnifying glass was slowly rotated in the light over the design for 5 seconds; the paper was moved slightly and the exposure repeated for 5 more seconds. Developed in Selectol.

40 A thin (⅛″) slice of lemon was put on a glass sheet and placed in an enlarger, printed at f/11 for 5 seconds on Velour VB 2 paper; developed in Kodagraph.

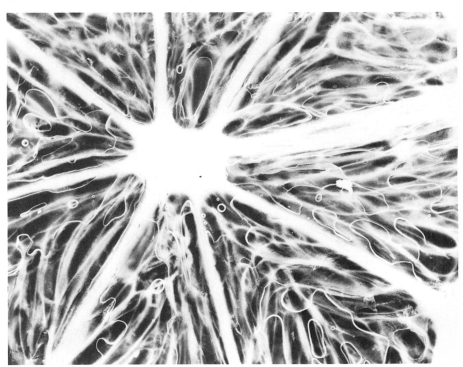

41 *Leaves and evergreen twigs were arranged on Agfa 2 paper and covered with a glass sheet to improve contact. A penlight, held in hand, was moved across the objects, exposing the paper; dark areas resulted from the light being close to the paper. The design was re-arranged several times during intervals in the exposure; developed in Selectol.*

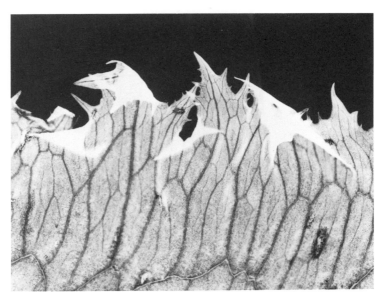

42 A lettuce leaf portion was put on a glass sheet, placed in the negative area of an enlarger and printed as a negative at f/11, for 4 seconds on Velour VB 2; developed in Kodagraph.

43 The design was made by arranging an electric lamp cord on Velour VB-R2 paper and exposing it with a penlight held in the hand at about 3 feet; exposures at three positions were for 5, 1 and 2 seconds.   Development was in Kodagraph.

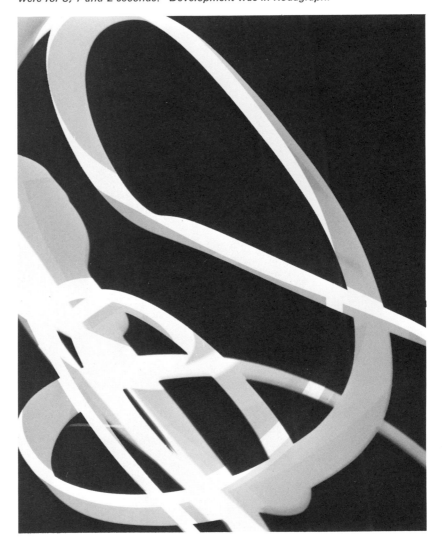

44 *A cut-glass dish was placed in the negative area of an enlarger and printed on Agfa F2 paper with three exposures: 14, 5 and 10 seconds; the paper was moved slightly between exposures. Development was in Selectol.*

45 *(opposite) Tissue paper and popcorn were arranged on a glass sheet for this light design, placed in the negative area of an enlarger and printed on Medalist F2 paper. Development was in Selectol.*

46 *Various objects including a comb, bobby pins and a rubber band, were used to make this design which was composed directly on Medalist F2 paper; exposure with an enlarger was at f/4.5 for two 10 second intervals between which the paper was moved slightly.*

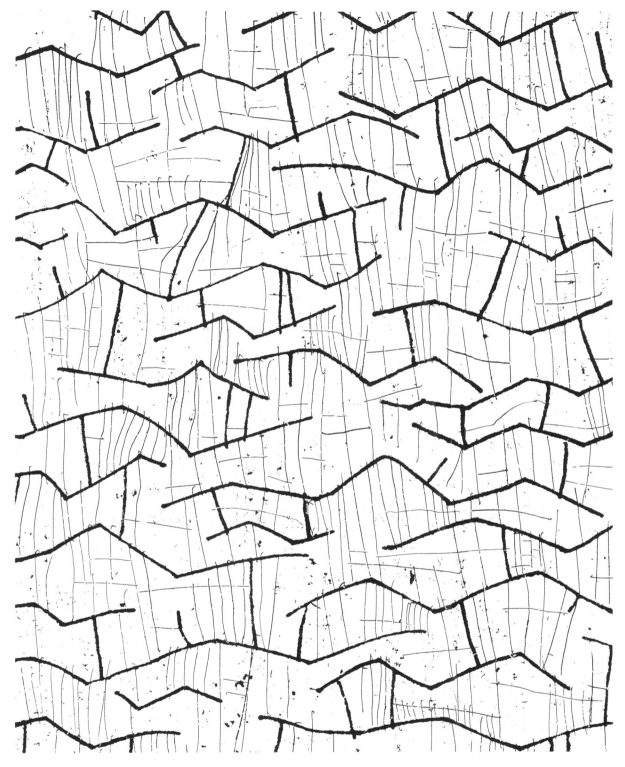

47 This design was drawn on paper with carbon paper in the usual copy position, which removed the carbon coating from the carbon paper. The carbon paper was placed face down on a sheet of acetate and carefully burnished, transferring the background (black) and leaving the design in white lines. The acetate sheet was used as a projection negative and printed. This technique is ready-made for making a design with repeated units.

Light designs with films (transparencies)

Light designs made with film have all of the qualities of those made with paper. In addition, prints on film may be reproduced (printed) for multiple copies, projected upon a screen or lighted from the back; for the latter use they may be mounted in double mats and hung with back-lighting or arranged in a light box.

For *roomlight* printing of light designs on film only a few materials are needed and the simplest of equipment is adequate for excellent results.

Materials

selected items with which to compose designs
film: EA4 (Kodak)
solutions: Kodak Dektol or Kodagraph developer
             stop bath
             fixer

Equipment

one reflector photoflood lamp (375 watts)
an extension cord with a lamp socket and a clamp
a timer, watch or clock
three plastic or enameled trays, 8" x 10" or larger, for solutions
three plastic or bamboo tongs (one for each solution)
a large tray or sink in which to rinse prints
glass bottles, ½ gallon or larger, in which to store solutions

As with certain photographic papers, selected films of low sensitivity to artificial light can be printed in ordinary roomlight without pre-exposing the film. Printing conventional films in the darkroom can be done in a contact printer or an enlarger, or light designs can be created directly on the film. A white light source is needed to make designs on unexposed film in roomlight or darkroom as discussed previously in reference to papers.

Objects selected for making light designs on film should have a variety of light reaction properties. Consider, for example, the contrasts in light and dark that can be produced with papers of different weights, fabrics of open or closed weave to create textures, and objects of metal and wood to provide solid shapes. Objects should also be selected for their properties of light diffusion as a cut glass tray. After collecting suitable items, one may find suggestions for arranging them in "Some Guidelines for Composing Light Designs."

48 *Students expose their light designs on EA4 film. Note the photoflood lamp at the top of the picture, the white light source placed 30" from the film; exposure time: 2 minutes.*

Roomlight printing with film

Unexpected as it may be, it is possible to use certain light sensitive films in roomlight conditions rather than in a darkroom. Light designs made on film in roomlight have the distinct advantage or requiring a minimum of equipment for satisfactory results. Kodak Film EA4[1] can be handled in normal roomlight up to approximately ten minutes without exposing it. Film, nevertheless, should be kept in the packing container until use to insure the best possible results in printing.

Exposure of Kodak EA4, tan side up, with one photoflood lamp at approximately thirty-six inches takes one to three minutes. In Print 48 students are exposing their designs in roomlight, a process which requires only glass sheets (edges taped) on which designs are placed, a photoflood lamp and a timer. Other students and their teacher are shown in Print 49, having used the same equipment, discussing their light designs.

Development of the film follows exposure and is the same process used in printing on paper. Three trays and three solutions are needed and arranged as follows:

Tray No. 1	Tray No. 2	Tray No. 3
Developer	Stop Bath	Fixer

The developer is Kodak Dektol or Kodagraph, the stop bath is 28% acetic acid (1 ½ ounces to 32 ounces of water) and Kodak fixer. Directions for mixing the developers and the fixer are on their respective containers. All solutions are used at temperature about 68°F.

To develop the film: Slip the exposed film face up into the developer, keeping it under the surface and gently agitating it with tongs. Traces of the design should emerge in a few seconds, it should be finished and ready to remove from the developer solution in fifteen to thirty seconds. Using tongs, hold the film print by one corner over the developer and allow it to drip, then quickly slip it into the stop bath solution for five seconds. Use different tongs in each tray so as not to mix the solutions. Place the film in the fixer solution for ten minutes with frequent agitation. Wash the print by placing it in a large tray of cool running water for thirty minutes; move prints around to insure thorough washing. Tray siphons may be purchased for washing prints, or water from the faucet may run into a glass tumbler

[1]This film is available from Business Systems Markets Division, Eastman Kodak Company, Rochester, N.Y. 14650.

49 *Students and their art teacher, second from left, discussing light designs which have been placed on papers to dry.*

and overflow into the tray not contacting the prints directly. Film prints may then be dried on paper towels or blotters.

In Print 50 a student is removing his print on film from the stop bath, following development in the tray on the right; next the print will be placed in the fixer solution on the left.

The·following light designs on film, Prints 51 through 61, were all made in roomlight conditions. Light designs on film may be placed between glass sheets, framed and hung with natural or artificial light coming from behind, as in Print 58.

Multiple prints may be required to produce repeated designs (single unit, border or all-over.) In roomlight printing the most distinct prints result from direct printing of the original design set-up rather than from the use of a negative or positive transparency. Print 59 shows a design set-up made of metal and wood strips and pieces of stained glass all of which have been taped to a sheet of clear glass (note design area within black lines.) Prints from this design set-up were used to make the single unit design in Print 60 and the border design in Print 78. The latter is shown mounted in a double mat which permits back lighting to illuminate the design, thus exploiting translucent characteristics of the film.

Print 61 illustrates a light box made of wood and containing a 15 watt fluorescent lamp which provides back-light illumination for prints made in roomlight on EA4 film. The prints were placed between glass sheets and mounted in windows of the box.

50 *(left) A light design, printed on EA4, is being removed by a student from stop bath solution. Dektol developer is in the tray on the right; fixer solution is to the left.*

44

51 (above-left) Coins, sticks, thread and window screen are arranged to make this light design on EA4 film.

52 (above-right) Hands are the subject of this composition on EA4 film.

53 (below-right) A square metal piece and other objects make this light design on EA4 film.

54/55/56 *Various objects are composed for light designs which were printed on EA4 film with a photoflood lamp at 36''; exposure time: 2 minutes.*

46

57 *(above) Two prints on EA4 film are overlaid to make this light design.*

58 *(opposite) Three prints on EA4 film are placed between 4'' x 5'' glass sheets and mounted in a wood frame which may be hung at a window for back lighting. Over-all dimensions: 4¾'' x 24''.*

63 By projecting through burlap cloth a coarse texture was created on Adlux film. Washes with black ink and a form in red ink introduce additional textures and a center of focus to develop the design.

be considered. Another technique is to place these objects on a glass sheet and position it over the film for exposure. Exposure time may vary from four to twelve seconds or longer depending on the density of the design objects, distance from the enlarger lamp to the film and whether or not the film is moved during exposure.

The development of Adlux film is as follows:

Tray No. 1	Tray No. 2	Tray No. 3
53D (DuPont) or	Stop Bath	Fixer
Versatol Developer (1:3)	8–10 seconds	8–10 *minutes*
10–60 seconds		

Washing follows fixing and is done in rapidly changing cool water, as described earlier in this section, for twenty minutes. To dry, gently wipe both sides of the film with a clean cellulose sponge and place it on paper towels or blotters, or hang in a dust-free location.

Prints 62 through 66 were made with Adlux film. In some designs selected materials were included to add texture and color. The projection of these transparencies (slides) changes their scale, through enlargement, and transforms them when light penetrates the transparent elements. These illustrations serve, then, as approximations of the projected image. Note the captions for a description of each print.

Print 66 illustrates light designs on Adlux which were placed between 4'' x 5'' glass sheets and mounted in a light box with back illumination. Some of these designs were brightened with color by drawing on the film with ink or pencil or by adding cellophane and tissue paper shapes.

Light designs on film also may be viewed on a wall screen with a 35mm or larger projector or with an overhead projector.

52

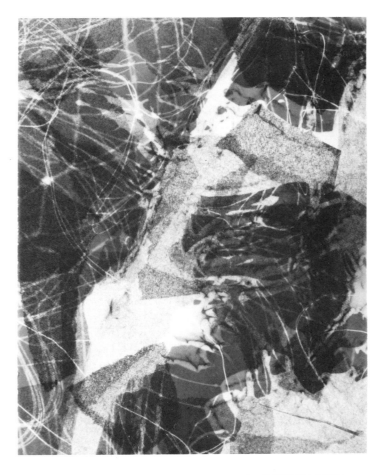

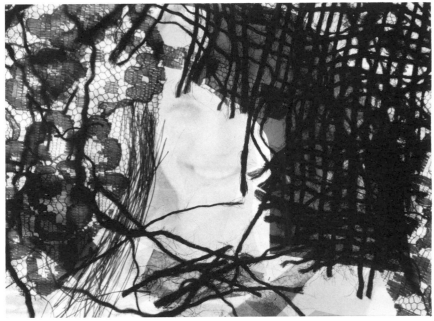

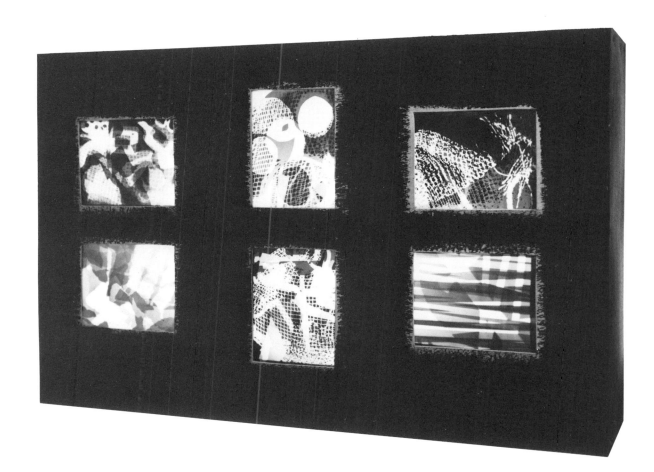

64 (opposite-top) A background of lines was created with fine wires and other materials on Adlux film which was overlaid with tissue paper shapes, some overlapping, combining to create a subtle light design.

65 (opposite-bottom) Using a photo-transparency for the central area of this design (titled "Sweet Sixteen,") other materials which develop the theme were added to the composition.

66 (above) A light box, 6"d x 15"h x 24"w, made of cardboard on a wood frame, containing two 25 watt bulbs for back lighting of the six Adlux prints. A sheet of frosted plastic, placed between the bulbs and the prints, serves to diffuse the light.

54

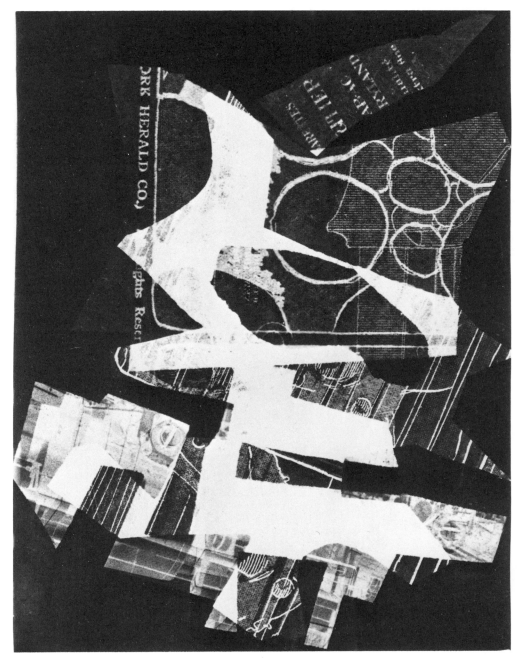

67 *Christian Schad: Schadograph, 1918; Permission the artist.   Collection The Museum of Modern Art, New York City, Anonymous Gift*

68 *(opposite) Laszlo Maholy-Nagy: Photogram, c. 1940; Permission Sibyl Maholy-Nagy. The George Eastman House Collection, Rochester, New York*

A selection of light designs

The light designs shown in this section, from widely separated sources, were selected for their compositional and technical qualitites.   Represented here is a variety of subject matter content.

Uniqueness and individuality are integral characteristics of each print and serve to illustrate the immeasurable versatility of the medium of light designs.

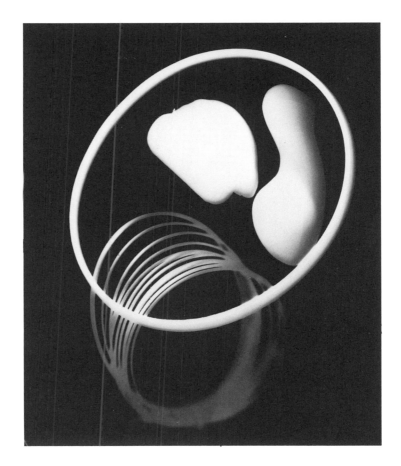

56

69 Francis Bruguiere: Design Based On a Question Mark, 1929; Permission Rosalind Fuller, M.B.E.   The George Eastman House Collection, Rochester, New York

70 (opposite) Man Ray: Rayograph, 1927; Permission the artist.   The George Eastman House Collection, Rochester, New York

Man Ray 1927

72 *Man Ray: Rayograph, 1938; Permission the artist. The George Eastman House Collection, Rochester, New York*

73 *(opposite) Lotte Jacobi: One of a Series of Photogenics, 1948–1959; Permission the artist. Collection The Museum of Modern Art, New York City*

74 *(below) Henry W. Ray: Soot Patterned ⚹ 1, 1968; Permission the artist. Collection of the author.*

62

75 *Evelyn Knox Tarantino: Photogram, 1967.   Permission the artist*

76 *Sandra Etchells: Twig, 1968.   Permission the artist*

77 *Lawrence Dellolio: Portraits in Black, Grays, and White, 1968, (10" x 72").*
Permission the artist

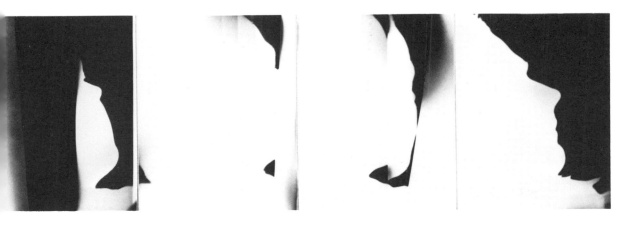

78 *Robert W. Cooke: Light Design ⌗ 10, 1968*

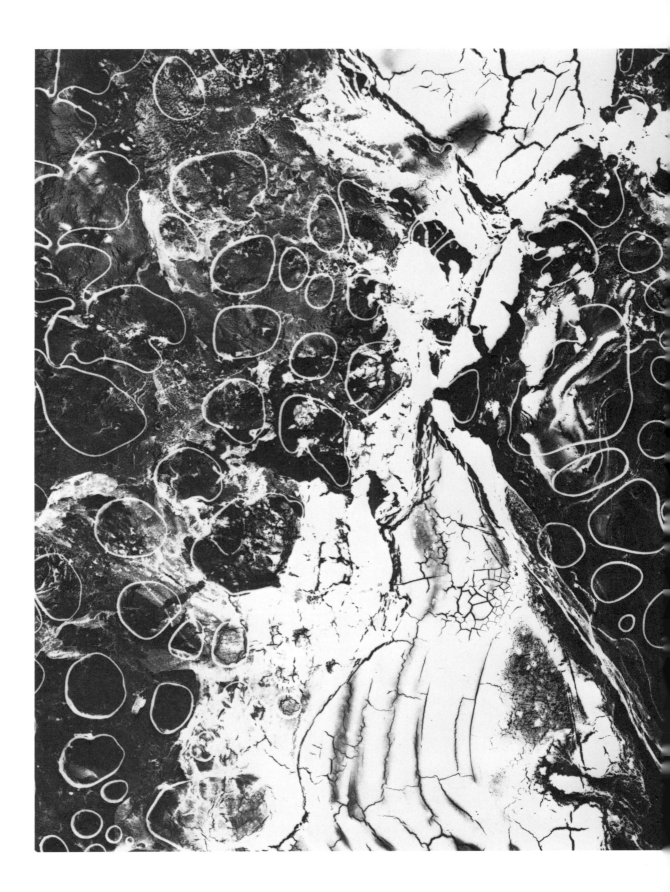

79 *(opposite) Jean Demetroulakos: Memory, 1968; Permission the artist*

80 *(below) Frank Mulvey: Untitled; Permission the artist*

68

81 Pauline Albenda: Found Sea Shells; Permission the artist

82 AT1 paper requires no exposure by light, only development and wiping away the black emulsion to create the design. The print was passed through stop bath, fixer and then washed as usual.

Experiments and ideas for designing with light

Light designs may be made with techniques long associated with photograms and previously described in this book, yet there are infinite possibilities awaiting discovery through experimentation. Searching for and developing new techniques are significant and engrossing aspects of creating light designs. However fascinating the search may be it is most important that emphasis be placed upon the resulting prints and transparencies and that innovative techniques and methods be only the means to this end.

A group of prints and transparencies are included here which illustrate a few of the endless possibilities for making light designs. To facilitate study of the processes, information as to how each one is made is included in the captions. These examples may suggest to the reader directions for further experimentation. Following the illustrated portion are additional written ideas.

Making experimental light designs in roomlight

It is possible to make dynamic designs without the usual exposure of papers and films. One of these methods is illustrated in Print 82, which was made with (Kodak) AT1 paper. Following development of the paper, and while it was still wet, the design was created by carefully wiping away portions of the black emulsion with a paper towel; *no* exposure was necessary.

Prints 83, 84, 85, 86, and 87 are examples of the possibilities in using pre-exposed 35mm color slides in which the design is applied directly to the film. A cotton swab containing a laundry bleach was used to clear the central portion of the slides. Compositions were made from selected materials and secured in place with a household cement. When dry the slide is ready to be projected on a wall screen.

Prints 88, 89 and 90 were made from colored cellophane and tissue papers sandwiched between two 3″ x 4″ glass sheets for projection or back-lighted mounting.

Prints made on film (slides, too) may be contact printed in roomlight as in Print 91 or enlarged. These prints may be used as units to make a repeated design.

83/84/85/86/87 Examples on this and facing page were made from pre-exposed color slides that were partially cleared by "erasing" the emulsion with a liquid laundry bleach (Clorox) on a cotton swab; small objects were attached with a clear household cement (Duco). Visual interest was created with transparent inks, dyes and felt tip markers.

70

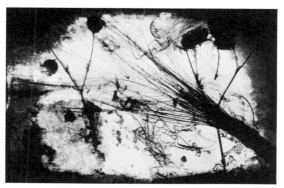

88/89/90 Two glass sheets (slides) 3¼'' x 4'', taped together at the edges, hold each light design of colored cellophane in place; may be projected or mounted and back-lighted.

91 *A contact print of a 3" x 4" light design transparency was made in roomlight on R1 paper by exposing it for three minutes with a 75 watt bulb in a desk lamp at 24".*
A good method for making multiple prints.

73

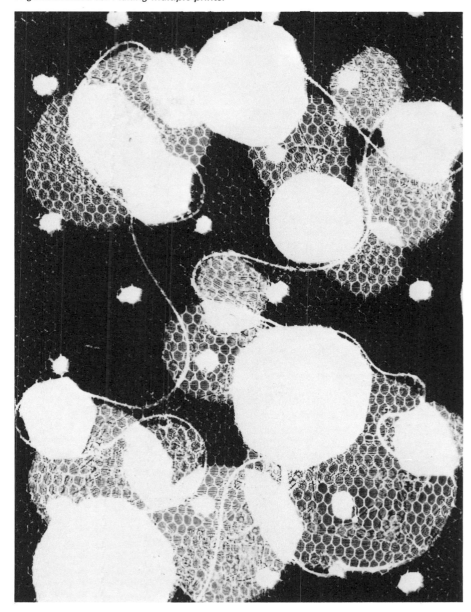

92 Cleansing powder was arranged on a glass sheet and printed as a projection negative.

*Experimental
light design
in a darkroom*

Using an enlarger, the following experimental light designs were made in the darkroom. Print 92 illustrates a way of controlling values and forms. A cleansing powder has been arranged on a glass sheet which was placed in an enlarger as a negative and printed on photographic paper.

Prints 93 and 94 show a design that has been sketched on clear film with a china marking pencil; a selected portion of the design was projected in an enlarger and printed.

Dripping developer on out-dated X-ray film, then softening the emulsion in hot water created the organic design in Print 95. An enlargement of a portion of the original is seen in Print 96.

A single match provided the illumination necessary to expose each of Prints 97 and 98.

Weathered glass fragments were placed on print paper and exposed in Print 99.

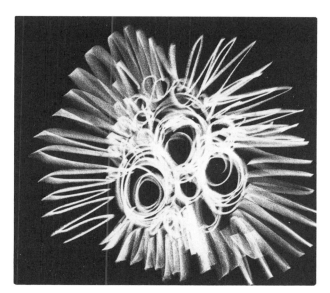

93 *A sketch with a china marking pencil was made on clear film.*

94 *A section of Print 93 was blown up with an enlarger. A good medium for drawing.*

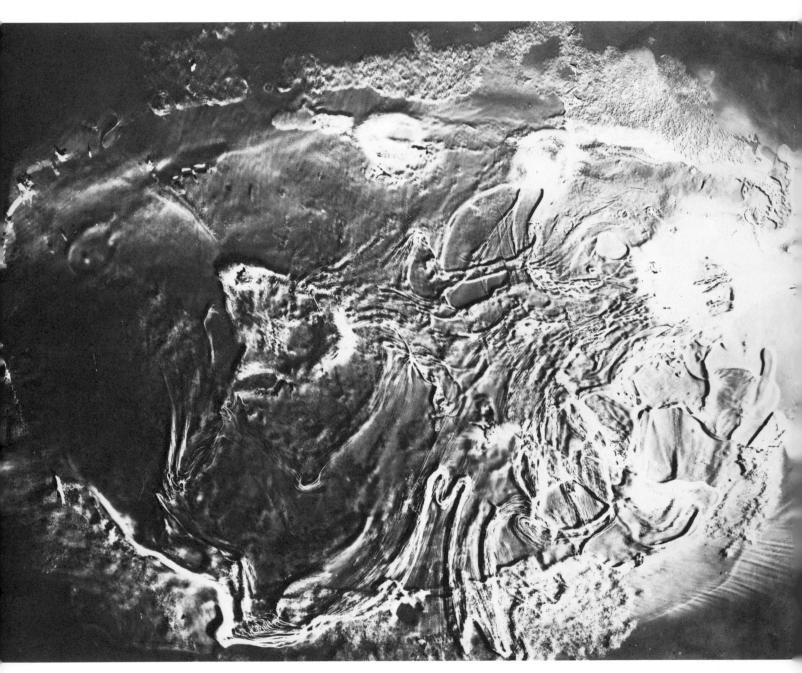

95 Developer solution in a medicine dropper was dropped on out-dated X-ray film which was then placed in hot water to soften the emulsion, followed by tilting the film to compose the organic design. The film was placed in stop bath, fixer and then washed, as usual.

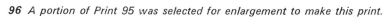

96 A portion of Print 95 was selected for enlargement to make this print.

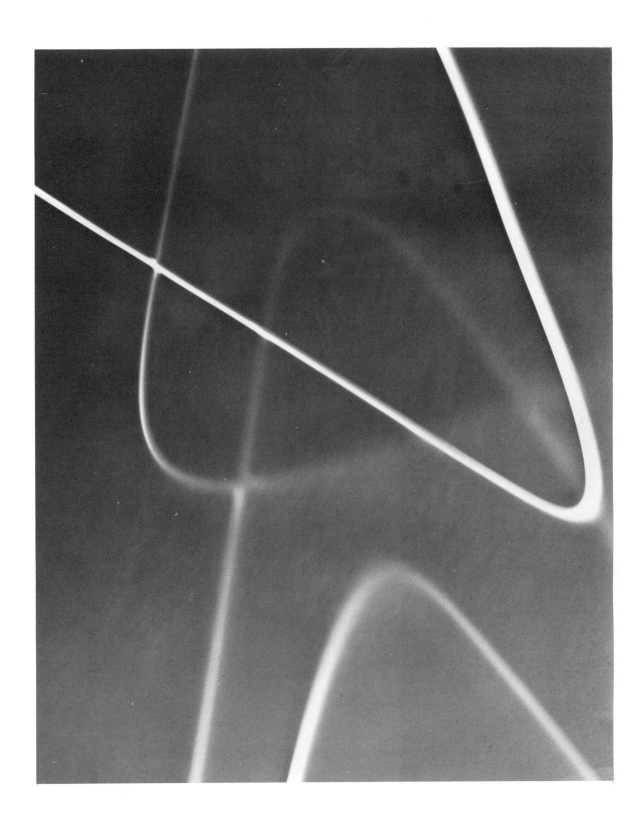

97 *(opposite) Bent wires made the white line design on Medalist F1 when the paper was exposed with a lighted match,*

98 *A looped electrical cord was positioned on the VB-R2 paper which was then exposed with a lighted match in slow movement.*

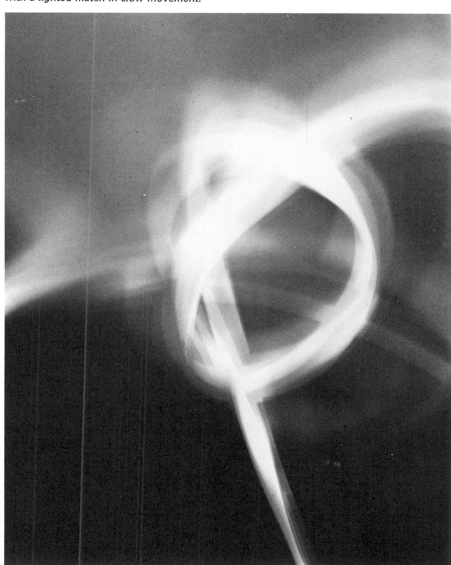

99 *Weathered glass fragments of different colors were placed on print paper and exposed to a light source.*

Additional ideas for experimentation

1 *Try* scratching a design into the emulsion side of black film (overexposed black and white film or unexposed color film.)   Use a sharp tool as a scratchboard blade; print by contact or enlarger, depending on size, or project on a wall screen.

2 *Try* another sgraffito (scratching) method, similar to the one above, by painting a sheet of glass with black paint and, when dry, scratching a design in it.   A variation of this method is to paint a design on a sheet of glass with translucent varnish and print by contact or enlarger using the glass sheet as a negative.   The painters Corot, Daubigny and Millet used this process in the 1850's; it is called "cliche verre."

3 *Try* using a thin section of styrofoam, the surface of which has been textured (i.e. by gentle poking with a pencil); print on film or paper with contact printer or enlarger.   A search for the most interesting areas, in terms of organization, will produce better designs than random printing.

4 *Try* for a "three-dimensional" effect by overlaying two transparencies of the same design, slightly out of register, taping in position and printing with contact or enlarger.   The two transparencies may be mounted and backlighted if of sufficient size.

5 *Try* making a light design by overlaying two carefully selected transparencies of different subjects each with somewhat fewer elements than would be best when used alone.   Complete as in D above.

6 *Try* soaking a negative in warm water, before it is placed in the fixer solution; then fix at about 68°F., wash and dry.   Some experimentation with water temperature, time in the water and handling of the negative (as tilting) may be necessary.   The successful result will be a negative covered with small wrinkles in the emulsion which prints out as a highly textured surface; this technique is called "reticulation."

7 *Try* applying a design to paper or film with developer in a brush or eyedropper; complete finishing in stop bath, fixer and washing.   A montage may be made by placing together a group of these designs as units to build a larger design.

8 *Try* a combination of positive and negative characteristics in one print as follows: Use a light weight paper (Kodak Fast Projection Extra Thin paper or single weight paper.)   During finishing in the darkroom remove the print from the developer after approximately 40–60 seconds and expose to white light for a few seconds, then return it to the developer and,

under safelight, complete finishing in stop bath, fixer and washing.   This technique is
called "solarization."   Successful prints will have a bas-relief effect.

9 *Try* for variations in values (grays) and sharpness by bending or curving the paper or
film in the enlarger while projecting the design.

10 *Try* sketching with pen and ink, a soft pencil or a china marking pencil on tracing paper
(or onion skin paper) and printing the sketch on paper or film.

11 *Try* combining black and white negatives by projecting parts of them, selected for
interesting form and texture, on enlarging paper.   Negatives may be trimmed, placed together in the enlarger and projected simultaneously, or the paper may be masked to receive   ·
the negatives separately.

12 *Try* projecting color slides or color positive transparencies on black and white enlarging
paper; see above method.   A soft paper, as (Kodak) Medalist No. 1 will translate a wide
range of colors into black, grays and white; conversely, a No. 5 hard paper will reproduce
a narrower range of values.   The black and white print will be negative.

13 *Try* placing objects directly on paper or film and expose them with a light source from
various positions.

14 *Try* making light design prints with cut and torn papers or other essentially flat objects
in a copying machine.

15 *Try* printing designs on *colored* projection papers; colors now available are red, yellow
and green.

Appendix

Papers

ITEM	MFGR*	WEIGHT	SIZE	QUANTITY	APPROX. PRICE†	HANDLING: roomlight darkroom
A1 Kodagraph Autopositive	Eastman Kodak Co.	ultra-thin	8 ½x11	100 sheets	$ 7.30	roomlight
R1 Kodagraph Repro-Negative	Eastman Kodak Co.	ultra-thin	8 ½x11	100 sheets	8.90	roomlight
AT1 Kodagraph Autopositive	Eastman Kodak Co.	translucent	8 ½x11	100 sheets	11.35	roomlight
Medalist	Eastman Kodak Co.	single weight	8x10	25 sheets	3.25	darkroom
Velour VB-R2	E.I. DuPont Co.	single weight	8x10	25 sheets	3.25	darkroom

Films

ITEM	MFGR	SIZE	QUANTITY	APPROX. PRICE	HANDLING: roomlight darkroom
EA4 Kodagraph	Eastman Kodak Co.	8 ½x11	50 sheets	$20.10	roomlight
Adlux	E.I. DuPont Co.	5x7	25 sheets	5.30	darkroom

*Eastman Kodak Company, Business Systems Markets Division, Rochester, New York 14650
E. I. DuPont De Nemours and Co. (Inc.), Photo Products Department, Wilmington, Delaware 19898
†Check with suppliers for current prices.

	ITEM	MANUFACTURER	USE	FOR*		QUANTITY	APPROX. PRICE
Chemicals	Kodak Dektol	Eastman Kodak Co.	developer	EA4 AT1 Medalist	A1 R1	1 gallon	$1.25
	Kodagraph Developer	Eastman Kodak Co.	developer	EA4 AT1	A1 R1	1 gallon	.85
	Kodak Versatol	Eastman Kodak Co.	developer	Adlux Medalist		1 quart	1.45
	53-D All-Purpose Developer	E. I. DuPont Co.	developer	Adlux		1 gallon	1.40
	Kodak Fixer	Eastman Kodak Co.	clear and harden	papers and films		1 gallon	.85
	28% acetic acid	E.K.C., others	stop developer action	papers and films		1 pint	.65

	ITEM	DESCRIPTION	APPROX. PRICE
Equipment	tongs	bamboo or plastic	$ .50
	reflector photoflood lamp	375 watts General Electric or Sylvania	1.65
	timer	minute intervals	4.00 up
	contact printer	5 x 7	40.00 up
	enlarger	2¼ x 3¼	60.00 up
	tray	plastic or enamel 8 x 10 or larger	1.00 up
	extension cord	with lamp socket and clamp	2.50
	dry mount tissue	150 sheets, 8 x 10	4.50

*This chart indicates the uses of these chemicals with reference to the work described in this book and follows the manufacturers' recommendations in most cases.

Glossary

The terms listed in the Glossary are defined within the context of this book.

Acetic Acid (28%). See "Stop Bath."

Adlux A photographic film for transparencies; use in the darkroom. (DuPont)

Agfa F2 A projection (enlarger) paper of normal grade; darkroom handling. Agfa-Gevaert Inc., Teterboro, New Jersey.

All purpose developer, 53-D A photo chemical for developing prints and negatives (DuPont)

Aperture The opening of a lens diaphragm regulating the amount of light which passes through it; either a camera or an enlarger lens. Aperture is indicated, with reference to lens focal length, by "f" as: F/3.5.

A1 paper Kodak autopositive paper, ultra-thin; roomlight handling.

AT1 paper Kodak autopositive paper, translucent.

Back lighting Light which originates from behind an object. See Prints 58 and 61.

Bas-relief A three-dimensional effect in a photographic negative resulting from a second exposure to white light during development. The double exposure produces positive and negative images on one negative. The term "solarization" refers to this darkroom technique, the results of which are largely unpredictable.

Camera obscura (dark chamber) A forerunner of the photographic camera; first a room, then a box with a small hole in one side through which an outside view was projected, inverted and on an opposite wall or side (1039?). The device was used by artists as an aid in sketching outdoor scenes (1558), later contained a lens with a mirror at 45 degrees to the line of sight, which reflected the subject onto a ground glass surface (1685). The camera obscura was converted to photographic uses by J. Nicephore Niépce (1826) who added a bellows and an iris diaphragm to sharpen the image.

Cellulose sponge A fine grain cellulose photographic sponge for use in wiping water from films when drying them to reduce the possibility of spots. (DuPont)

Cleansing powder Any powdered household enamel surface and tile cleaner as, for example "Comet" or "Ajax" brands.

Contact paper A photographic paper, one side of which is coated with silver chloride, used in making prints from a negative of the same size with a contact printer; light designs may be made with the printer, with or without a negative, or by placing objects directly on contact paper and exposing it with white light.

Contact printer A device designed for making prints from negatives of the same size in the darkroom, also used for making designs with light on paper or film by placing selected flat objects on its glass area (top), covering them with photographic paper or film, emulsion side down, and exposing the paper or film by turning on the printer's lamp for a few seconds. See Print 35.

Contact printing frame A sheet of clear glass in a frame the back of which opens to permit the insertion of flat objects and paper or film to make a light design. The light-sensitive materials can be exposed with a 60 watt white electric light bulb at one or two feet for a few seconds. This device can be used in roomlight or in a darkroom depending upon the materials selected.

Copying machine An office copier as, for example, a "Xerox" machine.

Darkroom A room from which light is excluded, except for recommended safelights, where prints and films are developed and printed.

Darkroom handling A term referring to photographic materials which can be opened and worked with only in darkroom conditions. See "Roomlight."

Dektol A developer for prints and enlargements on cold-toned papers. (Kodak)

Density A term which refers to the light passing or blocking properties of objects used for making light designs.

Dry mounting tissue A thin sheet of heat-sensitive material used in mounting photographs on cardboard; used with an electric iron or a press made for this purpose.

EA4 Kodagraph autopositive film which is designed for roomlight handling. (Kodak)

Emulsion A deposit of light-sensitive chemicals (silver halides) on photographic papers and films held in suspension in gelatin. Under suitable conditions of exposure to light an image is formed in the emulsion.

Enlarger A device for making designs with light by placing selected objects in the negative (carrier) area or by placing them directly on sensitized paper or film and exposing them by turning on the enlarger lamp.

Fixer A chemical solution which clears prints and films of chemicals that cause stains; also hardens the surface (emulsion) to prevent scratches.

Fogging A haze of grayness on photographic paper and film which results from pre-exposure to light; a similar condition may also result from improper fixing.

Household cement A clear, fast drying and hard binder as, for example, "Duco" brand.

Kodagraph Developer One of several photographic developers manufactured for use with drawing reproduction films and papers. (Kodak)

Laundry bleach A liquid household laundry bleach as, for example, "Clorox" brand.

Light box A box (wood or cardboard) with openings in one or more sides for mounting light-designs on film which are backlighted by an electric lamp(s.) See Prints 61 and 66.

Light design A modernization of the term "photogram" (light drawing) used with reference to darkroom prints made by composing designs with two-dimensional objects directly on light-sensitive paper (Schad, 1918). Later designs were made with three-dimensional objects (Man Ray and L. Maholy-Nagy, 1921). Also called "cameraless photography". Contemporarily, compositions are made on papers and films in roomlight as well as in the darkroom to create light designs.

Light diffusion The scattering of light rays or causing them to be less direct by the imposition of an object between the source and the photo-sensitive surface upon which they fall. See Prints 38 and 44.

Medalist paper An enlarging (projection) paper available in several contrasts or grades. (Kodak)

Montage The combining of selected prints for making a composite design by cutting and mounting them together, or by sandwiching black and white negatives or color positives between glass for printing or projecting. The resulting design: a photomontage.

Photoflood reflector lamp A specially designed flood lamp of 375 watts, with a built-in reflector, used to produce illumination for photographic purposes.

Photogram See "Light Design."

Print dryer (electric) A device with a polished metal (chromium) surface, electrically warmed, which is used for rapid drying of photographic prints on paper. Papers with a "glossy" finish (i.e. Kodak "f") are placed with the emulsion side in direct contact with the metal surface. "Luster" and "matte" finish papers are dried by placing them with the emulsion side away from the metal surface, as may "glossy" papers for a dull finish.

Projection paper A photographic paper, coated with silver bromide, used in making light designs with an enlarger or selected objects may be placed directly on this paper, composed into a design and exposed with a white light. See "Enlarger."

R1 paper Kodagraph Repro-Negative paper, ultra-thin, which is designed for roomlight handling. (Kodak). See Print 33.

Roomlight A term which refers to photographic papers and films designed for use in normal lighting conditions rather than in a darkroom. See "Darkroom."

Safelight A lamp of low wattage and suitable color which is used for (reduced) illumination in the darkroom without exposing certain light-sensitive films and papers. Note manufacturers' recommendations for use of a safelight.

Selectol A developer for prints and enlargements on warm-toned papers. (Kodak)

Sensitivity The quality of papers and films with reference to their characteristics when exposed to light, which may be stated as follows: a photographic material of "low" sensitivity is less responsive to the effects of light than one of "high" sensitivity. Roomlight materials are less sensitive to normal light than are those which can be handled only in the darkroom.

Stop bath A solution of 28% acetic acid (1 ½ ounces to 32 ounces of water) which is used to stop the action of the developer solution in the processing of films and prints.

Timer A mechanical device used to measure time; one type "counts" seconds and another type signals minutes. Timers are electric or spring powered; the former type may be plugged into a contact printer or an enlarger to turn off the lamp automatically at a preset interval.

Tongs Plastic or bamboo "tweezers" which are used to remove prints and films from solutions during developing, rinsing and fixing; one set of tongs for each solution. Fingers should be kept out of solutions.

Tray A square or rectangular, shallow container made of plastic or enameled metal. Three are used to hold photographic chemicals for processing films and papers.

Tray siphon A device used for washing prints and films, which directs water from a faucet in and out of a tray (set in or adjacent to a sink) while maintaining a constant high water level. Water, so directed, does not rush onto photographic materials and damage their emulsions.

Values This term refers to the scale of values, which are the grays between white and black. Values are produced in pigment by mixing black and white paints and in photography by the action of light upon the silver halides on papers and films; the more intense the light the darker the values and vice-versa.

Velour paper Velour VB-R2, a projection (enlarging) paper of normal contrast. (DuPont)

Versatol An all-purpose developer of films and prints. (Kodak)

Bibliography

Bevlin, Marjorie Elliott, *Design Through Discovery,* New York, N.Y.: Holt, Rinehart and Winston, Inc., 1963

Bruce, Helen Finn, *Your Guide to Photography,* New York, N.Y.: Barnes and Noble, Inc., 1965

Feininger, Andreas, *The Complete Photographer,* Englewood Cliffs, N.J.: Prentice-Hall, Inc., third printing 1966

Gernsheim, Helmut and Alison, *Creative Photography 1826 to the Present,* Detroit, Mich.: Wayne State University Press, 1963

Larmore, Lewis, *Introduction to Photographic Principles,* New York, N.Y.: Dover Publications, Inc., revised 1965

Lyons, Nathan, ed., *Photographers on Photography,* Englewood Cliffs, N.J.: Prentice-Hall, Inc., 1963

Newhall, Beaumont, *The History of Photography,* New York, N.Y.: The Museum of Modern Art, 1964

Latent Image, Garden City, N.Y.: Doubleday and Co., Inc., 1967

"Photograms," *The Focal Encyclopedia of Photography* (desk ed. 1962), New York, N.Y.: The Macmillan Company

Scharf, Aaron, *Creative Photography,* New York, N.Y.: Reinhold Publishing Corp., 1965

Picture credits

DESIGNING WITH LIGHT ON PAPER

11, 13, 14, 17, 20, 21, 22, 23 Rand School, Grade 6, Montclair, New Jersey Public Schools

12, 29, 30, 31, 32 High School, Mahwah, New Jersey; Francine Raia Buss, Art Teacher

15, 16, 18, 19 Pines Lake School, Grade 4, Wayne, New Jersey; Claire Donadt, Teacher

24, 25, 26, 27, 28 Hardyston Township School, Franklin, New Jersey; Judy Stolk Malinchak, Art Teacher

37, 38, 39, 40, 41, 42, 43, 44 Judy Stolk Malinchak

45 Jean Demetroulakos, College Student

46 Evelyn Knox Tarantino, College Student

47 Frank Mulvey, Associate Professor of Art, Sir George Williams University, Montreal, Quebec

11, 14 Sarita Rainey, Art Supervisor, Montclair, New Jersey Public Schools

12, 15, 16, 35, 36 Photocraft, Ramsey, New Jersey

13, 17, 33, 34 The Author

DESIGNING WITH LIGHT ON FILM

51, 52, 53 Rand School, Grade 6, Montclair, New Jersey Public Schools

54, 55, 56, 57 High School, Mahwah, New Jersey

62 Sandra Etchells, College Student

63 Lawrence Dellolio, College Student

64 Alan Sponzilli, College Student

65 Doris Muller, College Student

49, 50, 58, 60, 61, 62, 66 Photocraft, Ramsey, New Jersey

48, 58, 59, 60, 61 The Author

66, College Students

EXPERIMENTS AND IDEAS FOR DESIGNING WITH LIGHT

82, 92, 93, 94, 97, 98 Hardyston Township School, Franklin, New Jersey; Judy Stolk Malinchak, Art Teacher

83, 84, 85 Junior High School, Salem, New Jersey; Doris Bryant, Art Teacher

86, 87 Carlton School, Penns Grove, New Jersey; Roxanna L. Hurst, Art Teacher

88, 89, 90 High School Students; Roxanne Bruno Indovino, Art Teacher

91 The Author

95, 96 Dr. Henry W. Ray, Director Teaching/Learning Resources, Centennial Schools, Warminster, Pennsylvania

99 Frank Mulvey, Associate Professor of Art, Sir George Williams University, Montreal, Quebec